ELIZABETH
DAVID

PEPERONATA AND
OTHER ITALIAN DISHES

PENGUIN BOOKS

PENGUIN BOOKS

Published by the Penguin Group. Penguin Books Ltd, 27 Wrights Lane, London
W8 5TZ, England. Penguin Books USA Inc., 375 Hudson Street, New York,
New York 10014, USA. Penguin Books Australia Ltd, Ringwood, Victoria, Australia.
Penguin Books Canada Ltd, 10 Alcorn Avenue, Toronto, Ontario, Canada M4V 3B2.
Penguin Books (NZ) Ltd, 182 – 190 Wairau Road, Auckland 10, New Zealand · Penguin
Books Ltd, Registered Offices: Harmondsworth, Middlesex, England · This
selection is from *A Book of Mediterranean Food* (first published by John Lehmann
Ltd 1950), published in Penguin Books 1955, *Italian Food* (first published by Mac-
donald 1954), published in Penguin Books 1963, *Summer Cooking* (first published
by Museum Press 1955), published in Penguin Books 1965, *An Omelette and a Glass
of Wine* (first published by Robert Hale Ltd 1984), published in Penguin Books
1986. This edition published 1996 · Copyright © Elizabeth David, 1958, 1954, 1955,
1984. This selection copyright © the Estate of Elizabeth David, 1996. All rights
reserved · Typeset by Rowland Phototypesetting Ltd, Bury St Edmunds, Suffolk.
Printed in England by Clays Ltd, St Ives plc · Except in the United States of
America, this book is sold subject to the condition that it shall not, by way of
trade or otherwise, be lent, re-sold, hired out, or otherwise circulated without the
publisher's prior consent in any form of binding or cover other than that in which
it is published and without a similar condition including this condition being imposed
on the subsequent purchaser · 10 9 8 7 6 5 4 3

CONTENTS

iii

Soups and Hors d'Oeuvres

ANTIPASTI

Among Italian antipasti (hors d'oeuvre) are to be found some of the most successful culinary achievements in European cooking. Most midday meals in Italy start with some small dish of antipasti, particularly if the meal is to be without pasta. The most common antipasti are some kind of *salame* sausage, olives, anchovies, ham, small artichokes in oil, *funghi* in vinegar (rather tasteless and unsatisfactory, these last), pimentos in oil, raw fennel, raw broad beans.

Antipasti of fish, all kinds of small fry served in oil and vinegar sauces, as well as anchovies and the inevitable tunny fish, are at their best in Italy. Prawns, scampi, shrimps, *seppie*, *calamaretti*, *totani*, *moscardini* (the last four are of the squid family), mussels, clams, sea dates, sea truffles, oysters, crabs, cold sturgeon in oil, all appear on the hors d'oeuvre tray.

Vegetables are presented in a number of ways and there are plenty of ideas from which we could borrow. It is the unexpected which makes the charm of many of these little dishes: papery slices of raw artichokes; anchovies garnishing a salad of raw mushrooms; slices of gruyère cheese with crisp fennel or rounds of uncooked pimento; salty sheep's milk cheese with raw broad beans; tunny fish with cooked french beans; an unorthodox mixture of cooked mushrooms and prawns in a tomato-flavoured mayonnaise; cooked artichoke hearts, mixed into a salad of green peas, broad beans, and potatoes; tunny fish encased in rolled-up red peppers. To the enterprising there is no limit to the number of dishes with which, without overdoing the mixtures, a promising start to a meal may be contrived.

ZUPPA CREMA DI PISELLI

(Fresh Green Pea Soup)

A small onion, a slice of ham, a stick of celery with the leaves, 12 oz of green peas (weighed when shelled; about 2 lb in the pod), butter, a pint of water, about ½ cupful of milk.

Melt the chopped onion in the butter, then add the chopped ham and the celery. After 5 minutes put in the shelled peas, and let them get thoroughly impregnated with the butter before adding the water. Simmer gently until the peas are thoroughly cooked. Put the whole contents of the pan through the food mill.

Add the milk when the soup is heated up.

Enough for three.

MINESTRONE

¼ lb of dried haricot beans, 2 carrots, 2 small potatoes, a small turnip, 2 onions, a piece of celery, 4 tomatoes, half a small cabbage, 2 rashers of bacon, garlic, herbs and seasoning, olive oil, a small glassful of red wine, 2 oz of broken-up macaroni or spaghetti, or *pastine*, or any of the pasta made in small shapes, such as little stars, little shells, et cetera.

Put the haricot beans to soak overnight. Next day prepare all the vegetables, and melt the sliced onions in the oil, adding 2 cloves of garlic, the bacon cut into pieces, and plenty of herbs, marjoram, thyme, basil, or whatever may be available; add the chopped tomatoes, or a tablespoonful of concentrated tomato purée; pour in the red wine, let it bubble a minute or two, then add the drained haricot beans; cover them with 3 pints of hot water and let them boil steadily for 2 hours. Now put in the carrots and about 15 minutes later the turnip and potatoes. Ten minutes before serving, add the celery, the cabbage cut into strips and the pasta. See that the soup is properly seasoned, stir in 2 tablespoonfuls of grated Parmesan, and serve more Parmesan separately.

According to the season almost any vegetable can be added to a minestrone: peas, beans, spinach, leeks, small marrows; rice can be substituted for the pasta.

MINESTRONE GENOVESE

(Genoese Minestrone)

¼ lb of white haricot beans, 2 large aubergines, a cabbage, 1 lb of tomatoes, 2 or 3 small marrows or a piece of pumpkin, 3 oz of fresh mushrooms or a few dried mushrooms, 3 tablespoonfuls of oil, 3 oz of *pastine* or vermicelli, 2 tablespoonfuls of pesto (p. 45), grated Parmesan.

Boil the previously soaked haricot beans until they are three-quarters cooked. Strain them and put them into 3 pints of fresh water. Add the peeled aubergines cut into squares, the peeled and chopped tomatoes, all the other vegetables also cut into small pieces, and the olive oil. When the beans and the vegetables are all but cooked put in the pasta, and when it is tender stir in the pesto. See that there is sufficient seasoning, and serve with grated cheese.

The vegetables for this minestrone can naturally be varied according to the season; carrots, cauliflower, french beans, celery and potatoes can be added. The pesto makes Genoese minestrone one of the best of all.

ZUPPA PAVESE

Zuppa pavese appears regularly upon the menu of practically every restaurant in Italy. Rightly, for it is a capital invention, admirable when one is tired, and also for solitary meals, for it is not only quickly prepared but one dish provides the elements of a nourishing meal – broth, eggs, bread, cheese. You need chicken or meat or vegetable consommé. Naturally upon the flavour of the consommé depends the excellence of the result. You also need an egg per person, small slices of bread and grated cheese.

While the consommé is heating up fry your slices of bread (3 for each plate of soup) in butter. Poach the eggs in the hot consommé, lift them out into the heated plates, pour the consommé over them (through a fine strainer if there are any pieces of white of egg floating about). Spread a little grated cheese over each slice of fried bread, and arrange 3 round each egg. Serve more grated cheese separately.

Some Italian cooks break the eggs into the plates and simply pour the boiling consommé over them, but this method does not, to my mind, cook the eggs sufficiently.

PEPERONATA

One of the best Italian dishes of pimentos.
4 large red pimentos, 6 large tomatoes, 1 onion, butter and olive oil, garlic.

Cut the pimentos in half, remove the seeds and cut them into strips; skin and chop the tomatoes. Melt the sliced onion in a mixture of olive oil and butter. Add the pimentos and simmer, with the cover on the pan, for 15 minutes. Add the tomatoes, salt and a clove of garlic. Cook until both tomatoes and pimentos are quite soft and most of the oil absorbed. The mixture should be fairly dry. Peperonata can be eaten either hot or cold and it can also be reheated without spoiling. Add a little fresh basil when it is in season.

FAGIOLI TOSCANI COL TONNO

(Tuscan Beans with Tunny Fish)

The white beans, fat and tender, so beloved of all Tuscans, are not usually obtainable in this country, but good quality white haricot beans *can* be found.

Beans and tunny fish are one of the best known of Florentine dishes, and should be served in large helpings as a robust antipasto (no dainty little dishes with a spoonful of beans and a crumb or two of tunny).

Boil the beans (soaked overnight if they are dried) with plenty of water to cover them. They will take roughly 3 hours to cook. (If they are the new season's beans, which come into the shops here around early November, 1½ hours is often enough; 6 to 8 oz should be sufficient for 4 people for an hors d'oeuvre. Ask for cannellini or borlotti beans. The latter are fat, round, pinkish-brown in colour.) Add salt at the end. Strain them, add a few strips of raw onion, plentiful oil, and when they are cold put on the top a generous amount (i.e. the contents of a 6 to 8 oz tin) of the best-quality tinned tunny fish in oil, in large squares.

The Tuscans are, or were, much addicted to these beans, and even had a special flask-shaped earthenware pot called a *fagiolara* in which they were cooked over the open fire. The *fagiolara* was a beautiful and sturdy pot but it is now (1987) many years since I have seen one for sale. 7

INSALATA DI RISO E SCAMPI

(Salad of Rice and Scampi)

Cold rice makes an excellent first course. There should not be too much rice in proportion to other ingredients, it must on no account be overcooked, and it is best to season it while still hot.

Boil 1 cupful of rice in salted water. Drain it, season it with pepper, salt, nutmeg, plenty of olive oil and a little vinegar or lemon juice. Stir in a few shreds of raw onion. When it is cold, add a dozen cooked scampi or Dublin Bay prawns, a cupful of green peas cooked with shredded ham (as for *piselli alla romana*) and a handful of chopped parsley.

A rice salad can be made with any number of different ingredients: raw or cooked mushrooms, cold chicken, any shellfish, pine kernels, almonds, cooked or raw pimentos, celery, fennel, ham, olives. There should always be one crisp element to counteract the softness of the rice.

Pasta and Gnocchi, Pizza and Risotto

THE COOKING AND SERVING OF PASTA

In Italy the amount of pasta allowed for each person is 3–4 oz, whether homemade or dried. The latter is usually cooked in a large quantity of boiling salted water, say 6 quarts to 12 oz of pasta. It should be cooked *al dente*, that is, very slightly resistant, and it should be strained without delay. A warmed serving dish should be ready and the pasta should be eaten as soon as it has been prepared.

An alternative but little known way of cooking manufactured pasta is to calculate one litre or 1¾ pints of water to every 125 g or ¼ lb of dried pasta. Bring the water to the boil; add a tablespoon of salt for every 2 litres or half gallon of water. Ad the pasta. After it comes back to the boil let it continue boiling for 3 minutes. Turn off the heat, cover the saucepan with a towel and the lid, leave it for 5 to 8 minutes according to the thickness of the pasta, for example, 5 minutes for *spaghettini*, 8 for *maccheroni rigati* which are short tubes, ridged and thick. At the end of this time the pasta should be just *al dente*.

I learned this excellent method from the directions given on a packet of Agnesi pasta bought in the early 1970s. I find it infinitely preferable to the old-fashioned way.

The addition of a generous lump of butter left to melt on the top of the pasta as it is served, or of a little olive oil put into the heated dish before the cooked pasta is turned into it, are both valuable improvements. Whether the sauce is served separately or stirred into the pasta is a matter of taste.

LASAGNE VERDI AL FORNO

(Baked Green Lasagne)

Lasagne verdi are large strips of pasta coloured green with spinach. The Bolognese way of cooking them makes a rich and sustaining dish; a salad and fruit is about all one can eat after a good helping of lasagne. The proportions for *lasagne verdi* for six are: 1 lb of flour, 3 eggs, 3 oz (weighed when cooked) of purée of spinach, and 2 teaspoonfuls of salt. It is most important that the spinach should be very thoroughly drained before being mixed with the flour and eggs. Heap the flour up on the pastry board, make a well in the centre, break in the 3 eggs, add the salt. With the hands, fold the flour over the eggs and mix them thoroughly, then add the spinach. This paste must be thoroughly kneaded and worked, pushing it away from you on the board with the palms of the hands. It will be at least 10 minutes before the paste has attained the required elasticity. Now divide the paste into two pieces. Flour the board and the rolling pin, and roll out the dough again and again, stretching it as you do so round the rolling-pin, pulling it out thinner all the time, and lightly flouring the flattened paste between each rolling to keep it from sticking. By the time it has been rolled and pulled about twelve times it should be like a piece of cloth which you can fold or roll up in any way you please without its breaking. Put this prepared paste over a clean cloth on a table while you work the second half of the paste. When both are ready, cut them into pieces about half the size of an ordinary postcard.

Having ready a large pan of boiling water, throw in the *lasagne* and let them cook for 5 minutes. Drain them and put them into a bowl of cold salted water. You should have ready a *ragù Bolognese* and an equal quantity of very creamy béchamel sauce flavoured with nutmeg

(nutmeg plays an important part in Bolognese cooking). You also need a wide and fairly deep fireproof dish of earthenware, porcelain or copper, or a large cake tin. Butter it well and on the bottom put a first coating of *ragù*, then one of béchamel, then one of *lasagne*. Start again with the *ragù* and béchamel, and continue until the dish is filled, finishing with a layer of *ragù* with the béchamel on the top and a final generous coating of grated Parmesan cheese.

Put the dish into a previously heated but moderate oven for about 30 minutes. Keep an eye on it to see that the *lasagne* are not drying up, although it is inevitable that they will get slightly crisp around the edges of the dish.

A very adequate dish can be made from bought green *lasagne* or noodles as long as they are of good quality. But beware those English-made green noodles which are artificially coloured. The colour comes out in the water when you cook them. Check the list of ingredients before you buy a packet. The preliminary cooking will take 10–15 minutes instead of 5 minutes; otherwise proceed in the same manner.

SPAGHETTI ALLE VONGOLE

(Spaghetti with Clams and Tomato Sauce)

One of the regular dishes of Roman restaurants as well as of Naples and the southern coast.

Vongole are small clams, often unobtainable in England except in tins. Try using mussels or cockles, but fresh ones, not the lethally vinegared kind in jars.

For four people, buy 4 pints of cockles if they are in their shells, ½ lb if they are already cooked and shelled. If using mussels, allow 5 pints for four people.

Clean the shellfish carefully, scrubbing them first and leaving them under running water until all the grit and sand have disappeared. Put them into a pan over a fairly fast flame and let the shells open. Strain them. Remove the shells. In a little warmed olive oil, sauté a chopped onion and 2 or 3 cloves of garlic (more if you like). Add 1½ lb of chopped and skinned ripe tomatoes (or the contents of a 1 lb tin of Italian peeled tomatoes), and when this has been reduced somewhat, add the clams, cockles or mussels and a handful of chopped parsley. As soon as the shellfish are hot the sauce is ready. Pour it over the cooked spaghetti in the dish.

Cheese is never served with *spaghetti alle vongole*.

If ready-cooked cockles are bought from a fishmonger, keep them in a colander under running water for as long as possible, for they are sure to be gritty and probably salty.

SPAGHETTI À LA SICILIENNE

Cook about ¾ lb of spaghetti in the usual way. Meanwhile make ready the following preparation: 4 rashers of bacon cut in large pieces, ¼ lb mushrooms, ½ lb chopped onions, 2 chopped cloves of garlic, a handful of stoned black olives and 4 anchovy fillets. First fry the onions crisp in fat, add all the other ingredients to the pan, with a handful of coarsely chopped parsley, and cook together for a few minutes. Have ready a hot serving dish into which you put a tablespoon of olive oil and when the spaghetti is cooked and drained put into the dish, stir round with the oil, pile the onion mixture on to the top in a thick layer and serve very hot, with grated Parmesan handed separately.

CHIOCCIOLE AL MASCARPONE E NOCE

(Pasta Shells with Cream Cheese and Walnuts)

Mascarpone is a pure, double-cream cheese made in Northern Italy, sometimes eaten with sugar and strawberries in the same way as the French Crémets and Coeur à la Crème. We have several varieties of double-cream cheese here. None has the finesse of mascarpone but there are one or two which make a most excellent sauce for pasta.

Boil 6 to 8 oz of pasta shells. Some are very hard and take as long as 20 minutes; and although they are small they need just as large a proportion of water for the cooking as other factory-made pasta.

The sauce is prepared as follows: in a fire-proof serving dish melt a lump of butter, and for 3 people 4 to 6 oz of double-cream cheese. It must just gently heat, not boil. Into this mixture put your cooked and drained pasta. Turn it round and round adding two or three spoonfuls of grated Parmesan. Add 2 oz or so (shelled weight) of roughly chopped walnuts. Serve more grated cheese separately.

This is an exquisite dish when well prepared but it is filling and rich, so a little goes a long way.

GNOCCHI DI PATATE

(Potato Gnocchi)

2 lb of potatoes, ½ lb of flour, 2 eggs, 1 oz of butter.

Make a purée of the cooked potatoes, as dry as possible. Mix in the flour, the butter and the eggs. Season with salt and pepper and knead to a dough.

Roll it out into long sausage-like rolls of the thickness of a finger. Cut into pieces about ¾ in long and in each of these little cylinders make a dent with the finger, lengthways, so that they become almost crescent shaped, like a curl of butter. Drop them one by one into a large pan of gently boiling salted water and cook them for about 3 minutes. When they float to the top they are done. Take them out of the pan with a perforated spoon and put them into a heated fireproof dish with butter and grated cheese. Leave them a minute or two in a warm oven and serve them either plain or with a chicken liver sauce or in the Genoese way with pesto or with a meat *sugo*.

GNOCCHI DI RICOTTA

(Cream Cheese Gnocchi)

½ lb of ricotta or double-cream cheese, 2 oz of butter, 4 tablespoonfuls of grated Parmesan, 2 eggs, 3 tablespoonfuls of flour, salt, pepper and nutmeg.

Sieve the cream cheese, stir in the softened butter, Parmesan, eggs and flour. Season with salt, pepper and nutmeg. Form into *gnocchi* about the size of a cork, roll them in flour. Poach them in gently boiling water for 8–10 minutes. Lift them out and drain them when they rise to the top of the pan. Serve them with butter and grated cheese. Easier to make if the mixture is left to set for several hours, or overnight, in the refrigerator.

POLENTA

Polenta is finely ground Indian corn meal; it makes a filling but excellent dish and this is the recipe as it is cooked by northern Italians with large families to feed.

1 lb of polenta will feed 6 hungry people. First prepare a very large heavy pan full of boiling salted water; when the water boils pour in the polenta, little by little, stirring all the time to eliminate lumps and adding more salt and pepper. It will take about 30 minutes to cook, and when ready is the consistency of a thick purée (rather like a purée of dried peas) and is poured out on to a very large wooden board, where it should form a layer about a quarter of an inch thick. Over it is poured a hot and rich tomato or meat sauce which is topped with grated Parmesan cheese. The board is placed in the centre of the table and everybody helps himself. Whatever is left over is trimmed into squares about the size of a piece of toast and grilled over a very slow charcoal fire; the top crust of sauce and cheese remains undisturbed and the underside, being nearest the heat, is deliciously browned.

PIZZA

From the stuffy and steaming little bakers' shops of Naples and Southern Italy, where it still costs a few lire for a portion large enough for a horse, the Pizza Napoletana has travelled the world. In Paris restaurants, in Shaftesbury Avenue milk bars, in South Kensington coffee shops the pizza has become acclimatized. In the latest paperback thriller to come my way (*The Big Heat* by William McGovern), it figures as a delicate exchange of compliments, a token of esteem, between one hoodlum and another. The cheese-covered pizza arrives from Chicago by hand of hired killer in a foot-square wooden box, packed in dry ice. 'It's from Antonio's Cellar, ready for the oven.' The gangster is misty-eyed. 'Damn, this was a sweet thing for Sylvester to do – what a sweet guy.' He turns to his cook-valet. 'Get some Chianti tomorrow morning and we'll have a real Ginny lunch.'

Whatever there may be about a pizza which tugs at the heartstrings of a big shot of the Philadelphia underworld, to law-abiding British citizens I suspect that its chief charm is that thick layer of sticky melting cheese on the top. Whether it's on toast, or macaroni, or cauliflower, nearly everyone loves a nice top dressing of chewy bubbling cheese. But for those who may share my preference for one of the many versions of the pizza made without that rubbery cheese, such as the Provençal *pissaladière* or the beautifully named Ligurian *sardenara*, here is a recipe. Not for the hefty slab of dough thinly spread with onions or tomatoes and cooked on a huge iron sheet which you buy from the bakeries and which is food only for the really ravenous, but for a more polite, a household or *casalinga* version. In Italy many such recipes for the pizza have been evolved by chefs and household cooks; they use a basis of simplified brioche dough, or short crumbly pastry, or thin, miniature rounds of enriched bread dough no larger than a coffee saucer.

PIZZA SARDENARA CASALINGA

5 oz plain flour, 1½ oz butter, 1 egg, ½ oz yeast, salt, a little water.

Cut the softened butter in little pieces and rub it into the flour. Add a good pinch of salt. Make a well in the centre, put in the egg and yeast dissolved in about 2 tablespoons of barely tepid water. Mix and knead until the dough comes away clean from the sides of the bowl.

Shape into a ball, put on a floured plate, cover with a floured cloth and leave in a warm place to rise for 2 hours.

For the filling: 1 lb onions, ½ lb tomatoes, a dozen anchovy fillets (in San Remo, home of the *sardenara*, salted sardines are used), a dozen small, stoned black olives, pepper, salt, dried oregano or basil, and olive oil.

Heat 4 tablespoons of olive oil in a heavy frying pan. Put in the thinly sliced onions and cook them very gently, with the cover on the pan, until they are quite soft and pale golden. They must not fry or turn brown. Add the skinned tomatoes, the seasonings (plus garlic if you like) and the basil or oregano. Continue cooking until the tomatoes and onions are amalgamated and the water from the tomatoes evaporated.

When the dough has risen sprinkle it with flour and break it down again. Knead once more into a ball, which you place in the centre of an oiled, 8½- to 10-inch (21- to 25-cm) removable-base flan tin. With your knuckles press it gently but quickly outwards until it is spread right over the tin and all round the sides. Put in the filling. Make a criss-cross pattern over the top with the anchovies, then fill in with the olives. Leave to rise another 15 minutes. Stand the flan tin on a baking sheet and cook in the centre of a pre-heated oven at gas number 6, 400°F, for 20 minutes, then turn down to gas number 4, 350°F, and cook another 20 minutes.

(Alternative pizza or *pissaladière* filling: 1 onion, 2 cloves of garlic, 1 lb fresh tomatoes, 4 to 6 Italian tinned tomatoes and their juice, ½ coffee cup olive oil, dried basil or marjoram, seasonings, olives and anchovies.)

RICE

Rice is to the northern provinces of Italy (Lombardy, Piedmont and the Veneto) what pasta is to the south. I wish I knew who was the genius who first grasped the fact that Piedmontese rice was ideally suited to slow cooking and that its particular qualities would be best appreciated in what has become the famous Milanese risotto. The fact that this rice can be cooked contrary to all rules, slowly, in a small amount of liquid, and emerge in a perfect state of creaminess with a very slightly resistant core in each grain gives the risotto its particular character.

The Chinese, the Arabs, the Greeks, the Indians, the Spaniards, the Turks, the Persians, have their marvellous national rice dishes: spicy pilaffs, golden fried rice, lovely deep pots full of rice shining with oil, mountains of dry white flaky rice . . .

The Italian risotto is a dish of a totally different nature and unique. One comes across some odd directions in French and English cookery books as to the making of risotto. The rice is to be first boiled and then stewed in tomato sauce, one learns; or baked in the oven, or steamed, or even cooked with the addition of flour. (The French, curiously enough, have never really taken to rice cookery.)

In Italy rice is never served *with* chicken, meat or fish. These ingredients, if they are to be used, are always integrated *into* the dish. The one important exception to the rule is the *risotto Milanese*, always served with *ossi buchi*.

RISOTTO ALLA SBIRRAGLIA

(Chicken Risotto)

Half a boiling chicken, a small onion, 3 or 4 tomatoes, a piece of celery, a clove of garlic, a green or red pimento, a few dried mushrooms, a glassful of white wine, seasoning and herbs, a slice of ham or Bologna sausage, rice, butter, Parmesan cheese.

For four people use half a boiling chicken weighing about 3½ lb (the other half can be used for another meal). Remove the skin, take all the flesh off the bones and cut into fairly large, long slices. In a thick pan sauté the sliced onion in butter or oil and when it is golden add the pieces of chicken, the ham and the other vegetables. Let them fry for a few minutes, then pour in the wine, leaving it to bubble for 3 or 4 minutes. Add seasoning and fresh herbs (marjoram, thyme or basil). Add hot water barely to cover the contents of the pan, put on the lid and cook very slowly for about 2 hours, preferably in the oven. (This preparation can be made beforehand and heated when the time comes to make the risotto.)

For the risotto allow 2 good teacupfuls of rice for four people. In a large, shallow, and heavy pan heat 1 oz of butter or olive oil, and in it melt a small very finely sliced onion; add the rice and stir, allowing it to soak up the butter. Now add boiling water to cover the rice, stir again, and when the water is absorbed add more, cooking all the time over a moderate flame and stirring frequently so that the rice does not stick. Season with a little salt. When you see that the rice is all but cooked pour in the chicken mixture, sauce and all, and continue stirring until the liquid is absorbed and the rice tender. At this moment stir in 2 tablespoonfuls of grated Parmesan and 1 oz of butter. The risotto can be served in the pan in which it has cooked or it can be turned out on to a hot dish.

Most recipes for chicken risotto require a chicken stock made from the bones of the bird, but in this case the liquid from the previously stewed pieces of chicken supplies sufficient richness, so that it is really preferable to use water and reserve the carcass and bones of the chicken for a soup.

RISOTTO WITH MUSHROOMS

This is a very simple form of risotto and, needless to say, all sorts of things can be added – slices of chicken, sautéd chicken livers, beef marrow. It should also be noted that risotto is made with Italian rice, which is a round, absorbent variety; no other will serve the purpose so well, the long Patna type of rice being wasted on this dish, for it is not sufficiently absorbent and makes your risotto tough and brittle, whereas a poor quality or small-grained rice will turn into a pudding.

Take 2 cups of Italian rice, 2 pints of chicken stock, 1 medium onion chopped fine, 2 cloves of garlic, 1 wineglass of oil, ¼ lb of white mushrooms cut into slices. Into a heavy sauté pan put the oil and as soon as it is warm put in the onion, the garlic and the mushrooms. As soon as the onion begins to brown, add the rice and stir until it takes on a transparent look. This is the moment to start adding the stock, which should be kept just on the boil by the side of the fire. Pour in about 2 cups at a time and go on stirring and adding stock each time it has been absorbed. The whole process is done over a low flame and in about 45 to 50 minutes, the risotto should be ready. It should be creamy, homogeneous, but on no account reduced to porridge. One must be able to *taste* each grain of rice although it is not separated as in a pilaff. Grated Parmesan cheese is served with it and sometimes stirred in before bringing the risotto to the table. In any case a risotto must be eaten immediately it is ready and cannot be kept warm in the oven, steamed over a pan of boiling water or otherwise kept waiting.

SUPPLÌ

Supplì are rice croquettes containing in the centre a slice of mozzarella cheese and a piece of ham or mortadella sausage. They can be made most successfully with left-over risotto, and are so good that when making a risotto it is worth cooking enough to have about 2 cupfuls of rice left to make *supplì* the next day.

Stir 2 beaten eggs into the cooked rice to bind it. Take about 1 tablespoonful of the rice and put it flat on the palm of your hand; on the rice lay a little slice of ham and cheese. Place another tablespoonful of rice on the top of the ham and cheese and form it into a ball about the size of a small orange so that the ham and cheese are completely enclosed. Roll each *supplì* very carefully in fine breadcrumbs, then fry them in hot fat or oil, turning them over and round so that the whole of the outside is nicely browned. Drain them on to brown paper or kitchen paper. The cheese inside should be just melted, stretching into threads (to which the dish owes its nickname of *supplì al telefono*) as one cuts into the rice, so that a hard cheese such as gruyère is not suitable. An attractive dish for a first course at luncheon and liked by everybody. But it needs a deft hand.

Main Courses

VITELLO TONNATO

This is one of the standard summer dishes of restaurants all over Italy. The following recipe is from an Abruzzesi trattoria in Rome, where the *vitello tonnato* was particularly good, although not the classic version.

Make a good cupful of mayonnaise with 2 yolks of eggs, olive oil and lemon juice. Pound or sieve about 2 oz of best-quality tunny fish in oil and add this to the mayonnaise. Thin slightly with juice from the roast fillet of veal. Cut the cold fillet of veal (which should have been boned before cooking) into slices and pack it into a deep dish into which it will just fit. Pour the prepared sauce over and leave till next day.

This very delicate *vitello tonnato* is usually eaten as a light main dish, although in some regions of Italy, notably in Piedmont, it is commonly offered as a first course or antipasto.

ITALIAN FRICASSÉE OF CHICKEN

The breasts and livers of 2 tender chickens, an onion, parsley, 1 oz of pine kernels, 1 lb of new green peas, 2 cupfuls of chicken stock, a lemon, the yolks of 2 eggs, 1 oz of butter.

Melt the butter and soften the chopped onion in it without letting it brown. Add chopped parsley. Put in the chicken breasts (4 fillets to each bird) and let them fry golden on each side. Add the pounded pine nuts. Pour the hot stock over, put in the uncooked peas, and cook gently for 10–15 minutes until the peas are tender. Add the sliced livers and cook them for two or three minutes. Remove the fillets to a serving dish and stir a little of the liquor into the eggs beaten with the juice of the lemon. Return the mixture to the rest of the stock, stir till it thickens. It must not boil and the operation must be carried out quickly.

Serve if you like with rice.

FILETTI DI TACCHINO BOLOGNESE

(Turkey Breasts Fried with Ham, Cheese and White Truffles)

Cut the two sides of the breast of not too large a turkey into fillets. This is a very easy operation and from an 8 lb turkey you get 8–10 good-sized fillets. Flatten them out a little on a wooden board, season them with salt and pepper, and dust them very lightly with flour. Melt a generous amount of butter in a frying pan (if they are all to be done at once you will probably need to keep two pans going at the same time). Cook the fillets on both sides gently, for the butter must not blacken or burn. When they have cooked for 10 minutes place a slice of cooked ham on each fillet, a thin layer of mushrooms (instead of the white truffles which would be used in Bologna), finely sliced and previously cooked for 5 minutes in butter, and then a layer of grated Parmesan cheese of the best quality obtainable. Over each fillet pour a tablespoonful of chicken or turkey broth. Cover the pan. Proceed to cook very gently for another 7–10 minutes. Some of the cheese spreads, amalgamates with the butter and the stock in the pan, and forms a sauce. Serve quickly, for if the dish is kept waiting the sauce will dry up and the cheese will become hard.

ANITRA IN AGRODOLCE

(Duck in Sour-Sweet Sauce)

A duck weighing 4–5 lb, 2 large onions, 2 tablespoonfuls of sugar, a little fresh mint, 2 oz of butter, 2 tablespoonfuls of wine vinegar, a pinch of ground cloves, ¾ pint of meat or chicken broth or water, flour.

Slice the onions very thin and melt them in the heated butter and dripping. Season the duck with salt and pepper, roll it in flour and put it to brown with the onions. Add the ground cloves. When the duck is well browned pour over the heated broth or water, cover the pan and cook gently for 2–3 hours. Turn the duck over from time to time so that it cooks evenly. When it is tender remove it from the pan and keep it warm in the oven. Pour off as much fat as possible from the sauce and stir in the chopped mint (about 2 tablespoon-fuls). Have the sugar ready caramelized – that is, heated in a pan with a little water until it turns toffee-coloured. Stir this into the sauce and add the vinegar. See that the seasoning is right and serve the sauce separately as soon as it has acquired a thick syrup-like consistency.

This dish is also excellent cold. Instead of pouring off the fat before adding the mint, sugar and vinegar, make the sauce as directed and remove the fat – it makes the most delicious dripping – when the sauce is cold.

FEGATO ALLA VENEZIANA

(Venetian Calf's Liver)

A dish to be found all over Italy but at its best in Venice.

2 lb of onions, 1 lb of calf's liver, olive oil. Slice the onions very finely. Cover the bottom of a thick shallow pan with oil. When it is warmed, not smoking, put in the onions. They are to stew very gently, turning soft and golden yellow, not brown. Salt them lightly. When they are ready (about 30–40 minutes, cooked with the cover on the pan), add the prepared liver. This should ideally be the very tenderest calf's liver, so soft that you could put a finger through it as if it were bread. It should be cut in the thinnest possible slices, like little scraps of tissue paper, and it needs only a minute's cooking on each side. Serve as quickly as possible.

When obliged to use tough liver for this dish, have it cut as thinly as possible, but cook it slowly with the onions, for 10–15 minutes. It will still make an excellent dish, although it will not have the finesse of genuine *fegato alla Veneziana*.

OSSI BUCHI MILANESE

(Stewed Shin of Veal)

2 lb of shin of veal sawn into pieces 2 in thick, ¼ pint each of white wine and stock, ¾ lb of tomatoes, parsley, a lemon, a clove of garlic, 2 oz of butter.

In a wide shallow pan, brown the slices of shin of veal in the butter. Once browned, arrange them in the pan so that they remain upright, in order that the marrow in the bone may not fall out as the meat cooks. Pour the white wine over them, let it cook for 10 minutes, then add the skinned and chopped tomatoes. Let them reduce, then add the stock. Season. Cook for 1½ to 2 hours, keeping the pan covered for the first hour.

Prepare a handful of chopped parsley, a clove of garlic chopped and the grated peel of half a lemon. The Milanese call this mixture *gremolata* and it is an essential part of the traditional *ossi buchi Milanese*. It is to be sprinkled on the top of the *ossi buchi* before serving.

To make the dish as it should be, very tender veal from an animal not more than three months old should be used. A dish of *risotto Milanese* always accompanies *ossi buchi*.

Incidentally, I have seen it asserted that *ossi buchi* means drunken bones. It doesn't. It means bones with holes, or hollow-bones.

ARISTA FIORENTINA

(Florentine Roast Pork)

Remove the rind and, should there be an excessive amount, some of the fat from a piece of loin of pork weighing about 3–4 lb.

Press 2 or 3 cloves of garlic into the meat, with a few leaves of rosemary and 2 or 3 whole cloves. Rub the meat with salt and pepper and put it into a roasting pan with water, about 2 in deep. Cook it in a moderate oven in an open pan.

It will take somewhat longer than the normal method of roasting; allow about 45 minutes to the pound. The meat emerges tender and moist. Let it cool a little in its own juice, then pour off the liquid (don't throw this away – there will be good pork fat on the top when it has set) and serve the pork cold.

ARISTA PERUGINA

(Perugia Roast Pork)

The method is the same as for the *arista Fiorentina*, but instead of rosemary flavour the pork with fennel leaves and garlic, or if there are no fennel leaves available a few pieces of the fennel bulb or some fennel seeds. Although it is not orthodox, I find the flavour of the meat is greatly enhanced by rubbing the clove of garlic in a few crushed coriander seeds before putting them into the meat. One of my favourite recipes.

A nice accompaniment is a potato salad flavoured with a very little fennel.

CASOEULA

(Milanese Stewed Pork)

1½ lb lean pork, ½ lb of Italian pork sausage (*cotechino*, for example), a piece of pork or bacon rind, a white cabbage weighing 2–3 lb, 3 oz of fat bacon, ½ lb of carrots, an onion, a stick of celery, a bay leaf, salt, pepper, a tumblerful of white wine, a tablespoonful of flour, 1 oz of butter.

Melt the butter in a large and heavy pan and in it brown the chopped bacon, the sliced onion, the carrots cut into rounds and the celery into short lengths. Now add the pork cut into thick slices, the sausages (whole if they are small and cut into chunks if it is a *cotechino*) and the slice of pork rind.

Season with salt and pepper, add the bay leaf and sprinkle with the flour. Pour over the white wine. Cover the pan and cook very slowly. If there is too little liquid add a little stock or water.

While the meat is cooking clean the cabbage and cook it for 10 minutes in boiling salted water. Drain it, cut it into quarters and add it to the *casoeula* 30 minutes before it is to be served. The whole process should take 1½–2 hours, according to the quality of the meat. Slices of plain or fried polenta are served with the *casoeula*. Plenty for four people.

BRODETTO ALLA RAVENNATE

(Ravenna Fish Soup)

In the Marche and on the Adriatic coast fish soup is known as *brodetto*.

Several towns of the Adriatic coast, where the fish is notably good, have their versions of *brodetto*; those of Ancona and Rimini are well known, and another good one comes from Ravenna Marina. It is worth while, when visiting Ravenna, to drive the five miles to the Marina and to eat *brodetto* a few yards from where the fish has been landed, in sight of the long stretch of white sand and the pine wood where Lord Byron used to ride. After luncheon, if it is a fine day, go down to the port to see the fishing boats coming in with the day's catch; their sails are a fine patchwork of Adriatic colours, bright clear blues, rose reds, chrome yellow, faded green, cobalt violet; the nets are dyed black and slung between the masts to dry.

Here is the recipe for fish soup as it is made at Ravenna Marina. It must be left to the imagination and resourcefulness of the reader to devise something as good and beautiful with North Sea fish.

The fish to be used for the *brodetto* are two or three different varieties of squid (*seppie, calamaretti, calamaroni*), eel, red mullet, *spigola* (sea bass), sole and *cannocchie* (*squilla mantis*), a flat-tailed Adriatic and

Mediterranean crustacean with a delicate flavour and lilac marks on its white flesh. Also called *pannocchie* and *cicala di mare*.

First of all make the *brodo* or *sugo* (the broth, which is the basis of all Italian fish soups). Put the heads of the fish into a pan with parsley, pounded garlic, tomatoes, salt, pepper, oregano and a little vinegar. When the tomatoes and the fish are cooked, remove all the bones and sieve the broth. Keep aside this broth, which should be fairly thin and of a deep red-brown colour.

Into a wide shallow earthenware pan put some olive oil and parsley and garlic pounded together. When the oil is hot add a fair quantity of sauce made from fresh tomatoes and thinned with a little water. Put in the prepared and cleaned *seppie* for they must cook for a good 30 minutes before all the other fish, which are to be added at the appropriate moment, cut into thick slices. Cook them gently and without stirring or they will break – 30 minutes should be sufficient.

Remove them from their sauce, which will be nearly all absorbed by this time. Arrange them in a hot dish. Heat up the prepared *brodo* and in this put rounds of bread either fried in oil or baked in the oven.

The broth and the fish are handed round at the same time but in separate dishes, so that each person may help himself to the variety of fish he chooses.

It will be seen that, owing to the variety of fish required, it is pointless to attempt this soup for fewer than six or eight people.

TRIGLIE ALLA VENEZIANA

(Red Mullet Marinated in White Wine)

Put two leaves of fresh mint and a small piece of garlic inside each red mullet, medium-sized ones being best for the dish. Roll them in flour and fry them gently in oil; drain them and arrange them on a long dish. Prepare the following sauce. In a little oil sauté a small onion finely chopped; let it melt but not turn brown, then pour in about 6 oz of white wine and a tablespoonful of wine vinegar. Simmer the sauce for 10–15 minutes, until it has reduced by one third. When it has cooled, pour it over the red mullets. Serve them cold, garnished with a little parsley and slices of lemon or orange. Instead of frying the mullets, they can be scored across twice on each side and grilled, and the sauce then poured over them. They can also be eaten hot cooked in this way and are excellent.

PESCE MARINATO

(Marinated Fish)

In Italian cooking fish is sometimes marinated before being grilled or roasted. The fish is scored crosswise two or three times on each side. Oil, lemon juice and fresh herbs usually constitute the marinade, and while grilling the fish are brushed over from time to time with the mixture, a treatment which is a considerable help to a dry and flaky fish. Another way of serving fish is to fry them in oil, then marinate them for several hours in oil and white wine with the addition of chopped garlic, parsley and whatever fresh herbs may be available – marjoram, oregano, basil or mint.

Both these Italian systems could be beneficially adopted in England for the treatment of otherwise uninteresting fish.

SOGLIOLE ALLA PARMIGIANA

(Sole with Parmesan Cheese)

Have medium-sized soles, one for each person, skinned on both sides.
Lay them in a buttered flame-proof dish, well seasoned with salt and
pepper, and with more butter on the top. Let them brown gently and
turn them over so that they brown on the other side. Spread a thin
layer of grated Parmesan over the top of each and add a tablespoonful
of chicken or fish broth for each sole. Cover the pan and simmer slowly
for 5 minutes, until the soles are cooked through and the cheese melted.
Serve in the dish in which they have cooked, with halves of lemon
and a green salad. The cooking can be done in the oven instead of on
top of the stove. Made with fillets instead of the whole fish, this recipe
produces a splendid quick and unfussy little dish.

CALAMARETTI E SCAMPI ALLE STECCHE

(Inkfish and Scampi on Skewers)

The smallest, tenderest little *calamaretti*, soft as butter, are used for
this Adriatic coast dish, which is perfectly delicious.

The cleaned *calamaretti* and the shelled raw scampi are coated with
egg and breadcrumbs, impaled longways, end to end on green twigs
and fried golden in butter. Try it with scallops, the white parts cut
into two rounds, alternated with the red. They only take 5 minutes to
cook.

Vegetables and Sauces

NAVONI ALL' AGLIATA

(Turnips with Garlic Sauce)

A Genoese dish. Blanch the peeled turnips in boiling salted water for 5 minutes. Cut them in quarters and put them to stew gently in a small heavy pan with plenty of olive oil and season them with salt.

Prepare the *agliata* by pounding two or three cloves of garlic in a mortar and adding a very little vinegar. When the turnips are cooked, add this mixture to the turnips; stir well so that the garlic sauce is well amalgamated with the oil, add a little parsley and serve.

CAROTE AL MARSALA

(Carrots with Marsala)

Clean about 1½ lb of carrots and cut them in half lengthways, and then in half again. Cut out the woody part in the centre if they are old carrots. Melt 1 oz of butter in a sauté pan and put in the carrots. Turn them over and over so that they become impregnated with the butter. Season with pepper, a little salt, a little sugar, and a minute or two later pour in a small glassful of Marsala. Simmer for 5 minutes and then just cover the carrots with water. Put the lid on the pan and stew gently until the carrots are tender. Turn up the flame and let the liquid, which should already be considerably reduced, all but bubble away. The carrots should be shiny, with a little syrupy sauce. Garnish them with a scrap of cut parsley.

Marsala with carrots may sound an unsuitable combination. Try it and see. It is one of my favourite vegetable recipes. Good by itself or with any kind of lamb.

MELANZANE RIPIENE

(Stuffed Aubergines)

For the stuffing for 4 large aubergines you need about 4 oz of white bread without the crust, 8 anchovy fillets, a dozen black olives, a handful of parsley, 2 or 3 cloves of garlic, a tablespoonful of capers.

Cut the aubergines in half and scoop out about half the flesh. Chop this with all the rest of the ingredients, having first softened the bread with a little milk or water. Season with pepper and marjoram or oregano, but salt will probably not be necessary. Put the stuffing lightly back into the aubergines and arrange them in a baking dish. Pour a generous quantity of oil over them, cover the pan and cook in a slow oven for about an hour.

FAVE AL GUANCIALE

(Broad Beans and Bacon)

1½ lb of broad beans, 2 oz of bacon, 1 oz of butter, a small onion.

Put the chopped onion to melt in the heated butter. Add the chopped bacon. After 2 minutes add the shelled broad beans. Simmer for 5 minutes. Barely cover with water. Cook gently for 15–20 minutes. Add salt if necessary and a little pepper.

A favourite Roman dish.

CROCCHETTE DI SPINACI

(Spinach Croquettes)

To 1 lb of cooked, drained and chopped spinach add 1½ oz of grated Parmesan, nutmeg, salt, pepper, and 1 beaten egg. Form the mixture into small croquettes on a floured board, roll them in breadcrumbs and fry them in hot oil or dripping.

PISELLI AL PROSCIUTTO

(Green Peas and Ham)

The green peas which grow round about Rome are the most delicious I have ever tasted anywhere. Small, sweet, tender and very green, they are really best simply stewed in butter. Cooked in this way they make a most delicate sauce for finely cut homemade pasta, or for *riso in bianco*. The Romans adore these green peas cooked with ham. Try this method with young English green peas before they become wrinkled and floury.

2 lb of peas, a small onion, lard or butter, 3 oz of very good cooked ham cut into strips.

Melt the chopped onion in the lard or butter, and let it cook very gently, so that it softens without browning. Put in the shelled peas and a very little water. After 5 minutes add the ham. In another 5–10 minutes the peas should be ready.

Now for a dish which really brings out the charms of the sweeter white table wines of Italy, Florentine fennel. Perhaps it sounds freakish to suggest a sweet wine with a vegetable dish. But consider a moment. When the experts make a big production of choosing food to go with their wines, I wonder how often it is remembered that many vegetables are very sweet, that they quarrel badly with the claret chosen for the lamb, distort the burgundy with the game? Who stops to think that chestnuts, parsnips, peas, carrots, turnips, celery, Belgian endives, onions, even to a certain extent potatoes have potent overtones of sugar in their make-up which are intensified by the so-called classic French methods of cooking them to an almost caramelized state of sweetness. Think, for instance, of *navets glacés*, *carottes Vichy* and those small golden, syrupy onions which accompany so many French meat and chicken dishes. Delicious, but they don't help the red wine. Try these same vegetables as a separate course *after* the meat or fish, and you find that they almost take the place of a sweet or pudding. Mangetout peas are a good example. Their alternative name of sugar peas should provide sufficient indication of their qualities, and to me it is all wrong to muddle these exquisitely delicate and sweet vegetables with meat and potatoes, sauce and gravy. They should always be eaten as a separate course. With them try one of the naturally sweet wines of Italy, the ones they call *amabile* (soft rather than luscious or rich). They make a most interesting partnership with sweetish vegetables, perhaps even better than they do with a dessert dish proper for which they are not full enough. In fact the Lacrima Christi del Vesuvio, a wine which in the past I have not much appreciated, has proved quite a revelation to me when I have drunk it with a gratin of Florentine fennel. The two have a real affinity. This wine – which should be drunk chilled, but not with all the fragrance frozen out of it – is also very successful with dishes based on white cream cheese, either sweet or savoury. Italian cooking offers a rich variety of such dishes, the savoury ones often mixed with spinach, the sweet ones with cloves, nutmeg, cinnamon.

Orvieto amabile (the one in the flask), to my mind far more attractive and somehow more natural and right than the dry version, is a little sweeter than the Lacrima Christi, and makes a happy partnership with cooked dessert apples, or provides a nice finish to a meal when served with delicate little biscuits or cakes such as French madeleines. This wine should be well chilled.

Florentine fennel is a simple and refreshing vegetable dish, surprisingly not better known. It consists of the bulbous root stems of the Florentine or sweet fennel – this form of fennel now arrives in England from Israel, Kenya, Morocco, and sometimes from France and Italy, during the late summer and again in the very early spring. The sweet, aniseed-like flavour of the plant is not to everybody's taste but to those who do like it, it is quite an addiction.

For this dish allow a minimum of one large fennel bulb – for want of an alternative short name that is what everyone calls these root stems – per person. Other ingredients are butter, grated Parmesan cheese and breadcrumbs. Trim the bulbs by slicing off the top stalks, the thick base, and removing all the stringy outer layers of leaves. There is a good deal of waste. Slice the bulbs in half, longitudinally. Plunge them into a saucepan of boiling salted water. According to size they should cook for 7 to 10 minutes. When tender enough to be pierced fairly easily with a skewer, drain them.

Have ready a buttered gratin dish or the appropriate number of individual dishes. In this arrange the fennel halves, cut side down. Strew breadcrumbs over them (approximately 1 tablespoon per bulb), then grated Parmesan (again, 1 tablespoon per bulb) and finally a few

43

little knobs of butter. Put the gratin dish in a medium oven (gas number 4, 350°F) and leave for 10 to 15 minutes until the cheese and breadcrumbs are very pale gold and bubbling.

CIPOLLINE IN AGRODOLCE

(Sweet-Sour Onions)

1 lb of small onions, 2 tablespoonfuls each of olive oil and vinegar, a tablespoonful of sugar, 2 cloves, a bay leaf, salt.

Choose small pickling onions, as much as possible of the same size. Put them unpeeled into boiling water and cook them for 10 minutes. When they have cooled, peel them, put them in a pan with the heated olive oil, the bay leaf and cloves. Simmer them very gently for 5 minutes and add the vinegar and the sugar. Cook until the sauce turns to a syrup.

Can be served hot or cold.

CAVOLFIORE AL STRACINATI

Cavolfiore is the Italian for cauliflower and *stracinati* means, literally, pulled. Half cook a cauliflower in salted water; drain it, and discard the thick part of the stalk and the leaves, and divide the flowerets. Have ready a pan with warm olive oil in which you have put a clove of garlic chopped, and put in the cauliflower; mash it with a fork and turn it over and over until it is browned on all sides.

PESTO

A large bunch of fresh basil, garlic, a handful of pine nuts, a handful of grated Sardo or Parmesan cheese, about 2 oz of olive oil.

Pound the basil leaves (there should be about 2 oz when the stalks have been removed) in a mortar with one or two cloves of garlic, a little salt and the pine nuts. Add the cheese. (Sardo cheese is the pungent Sardinian ewe's milk cheese which is exported in large quantities to Genoa to make pesto. Parmesan and Sardo are sometimes used in equal quantities; or all Parmesan, which gives a milder flavour.)

When the pesto is a thick purée start adding the olive oil, a little at a time. Stir it steadily and see that it is amalgamating with the other ingredients, as the finished sauce should have the consistency of a creamed butter. If made in larger quantities, pesto may be stored in jars covered with a layer of olive oil.

This is the famous sauce which is eaten by the Genoese with all kinds of pasta, with gnocchi and as a flavouring for soups.

An imitation of this sauce can be made with parsley or sweet marjoram, and although the flavour is totally different, it is still good. Walnuts can be used instead of pine nuts, or nuts can be omitted altogether, but the result is a thinner sauce.

SALSA VERDE

(Green Sauce)

Oil, lemon juice, parsley, capers, garlic, salt and pepper, all mixed together as for a vinaigrette. There should be plenty of parsley and the sauce should be rather thick. Chopped anchovy fillets are sometimes added.

SALSA DI POMODORO

(Tomato Sauce)

Chop 2 lb of ripe tomatoes. Put them into a saucepan with 1 small onion, 1 carrot, 1 piece of celery and a little parsley, all finely chopped. Add salt, ground black pepper and a pinch of sugar. Simmer until the tomatoes have turned almost to a purée. Put the sauce through a sieve.

If a concentrated sauce is needed put the purée back in a saucepan and cook it again until the watery part of it has dried up. Before serving it with meat, fish or any kind of pasta add, when they are obtainable, a couple of fresh basil leaves.

RAGÙ

This is the true name of the Bolognese sauce which, in one form or another, has travelled round the world. In Bologna it is served mainly with *lasagne verdi*, but it can go with many other kinds of pasta. The ingredients to make enough sauce for six generous helpings of pasta are 8 oz of lean minced beef, 4 oz of chicken livers, 3 oz of uncooked ham 'both fat and lean', 1 carrot, 1 onion, 1 small piece of celery, 3 tablespoonfuls of concentrated tomato purée, 1 wineglassful of white wine, 2 wineglassfuls of stock or water, butter, salt and pepper, nutmeg.

Cut the bacon or ham into very small pieces and brown them gently in a small saucepan in about ½ oz of butter. Add the onion, the carrot and the celery, all finely chopped. When they have browned, put in the raw minced beef, and then turn it over and over so that it all browns evenly. Now add the chopped chicken livers, and after 2 or 3 minutes the tomato purée, and then the white wine. Season with salt (having regard to the relative saltiness of the ham or bacon), pepper and a scraping of nutmeg, and add the meat stock or water. Cover the pan and simmer the sauce very gently for 30–40 minutes. Some Bolognese cooks add at the last 1 cupful of cream or milk to the sauce, which makes it smoother. Another traditional variation is the addition of the ovarine or unlaid eggs which are found inside the hen, especially in the spring when the hens are laying. They are added at the same time as the chicken livers and form small golden globules when the sauce is finished. When the *ragù* is to be served with spaghetti or tagliatelle, mix it with the hot pasta in a heated dish so that the pasta is thoroughly impregnated with the sauce, and add a good piece of butter before serving. Hand the grated cheese separately.

This is the recipe given me by Zia Nerina, a splendid woman, titanic of proportion but angelic of face and manner, who in the 1950s owned and ran the Trattoria Nerina in Bologna. Zia Nerina's cooking was renowned far beyond the confines of her native city.

Sweets

GRANITA DI LIMONE

(Lemon Granita)

6 or 7 lemons (enough to produce ½ pint of juice), ¼ lb of sugar, 1 pint of water.

Make a syrup of the sugar and water by bringing them to the boil and boiling for 5 minutes. When the syrup is cold mix it with the lemon juice and freeze in the ice-tray of the refrigerator at the normal temperature for making ice. On account of the sugar the freezing will take about an hour more than the usual time taken for making ice.

Enough for six helpings.

GRANITA DI FRAGOLE

(Strawberry Granita)

Quantities are 2 lb of strawberries, the juice of half a lemon and of half an orange, ½ lb white sugar, ½ pint of water. Hull the strawberries, purée them in the blender, press them through a stainless steel wire or nylon sieve. (Tinned wire or tinned steel discolours the fruit.) Add the strained orange and lemon juice.

Boil the sugar and water for about seven minutes to make a thin syrup (to make a sorbet of greater density boil the syrup for 10 minutes or until it is beginning to thicken) and leave it to cool before adding it to the strawberry pulp.

Chill the mixture before freezing it.

As the name implies, this type of water ice should be slightly grainy, no more than just barely frozen. The quantities given should provide enough helpings for six to eight people.

APRICOT ICE-CREAM

1 lb of fresh apricots, 3 oz sugar, ¼ pint of double cream, water.

Halve and stone the apricots. Steam them until soft and sieve them. When cold add a syrup made from the sugar and ¼ pint of water simmered for 10 minutes. Immediately before freezing add the whipped cream. Freeze.

To make a firmer ice, the ice-cream can be cooked to a thin custard with the beaten yolks of 2 eggs. When cool, mix the apricot purée with its syrup into the cream caramel. Add also a few of the apricot kernels, skinned and crushed.

APRICOTINA

½ lb of dried apricots, ¼ lb butter, 2 oz sugar, 4 eggs.

Soak the apricots in water for 2 or 3 hours. Stew them slowly and keep aside 10 or so nice whole apricots for the garnish, and put the rest through a sieve, keeping the juice separately, and reserve 2 table-spoons of the purée, also for the garnish. Now put the purée into a saucepan, and add gradually the sugar, the butter and the yolks of the eggs, stirring all the time until you have a smooth thick cream. Leave it to cool. Fold in the stiffly beaten whites of the eggs and pour the whole mixture into a buttered soufflé dish and steam it (on the top of the stove) for 45 minutes. When it has cooled, turn the pudding out on to the serving dish. Now spread over the top the purée which you have reserved and on the top of this arrange the whole apricots. For the sauce, mix the apricot juice with an equal quantity of thin cream. This sweet is greatly improved by being made the day before and kept in the refrigerator, in which case it is preferable not to do the garnishing until an hour before you are going to serve it.

Apricotina is not such a trouble as it sounds; the result should be something between a moist cake and an iced soufflé.

FRESH FIGS WITH ORANGE JUICE

Allow two firm, very slightly under-ripe purple or green figs per person. Cut the stalks from the figs but do not peel them. Quarter them, put them in a bowl, and over them pour the juice, freshly squeezed, of one large orange for eight figs. No sugar is necessary, but the fruit should be prepared an hour or so before it is to be eaten.

Presented in a perfectly plain white china salad bowl, or in individual clear glass wine goblets, this fig salad is one of the most beautiful as well as one of the most exquisite of all fresh-fruit dishes.

PESCHE RIPIENE

(Stuffed Peaches)

6 yellow peaches, 3 oz of macaroons, 1 yolk of egg, 2 tablespoonfuls of sugar, 1 oz of butter.

Cut the peaches in half, take out the stones and a little of the pulp to make a deep space for the stuffing. Add this pulp to the pounded macaroons and stir in the other ingredients. Stuff the peaches with this mixture, spreading it in a smooth mound over each half. Put them in a buttered fireproof dish and bake in a moderate oven for about 30 minutes.

BUDINO DI RICOTTA

(Cream Cheese Pudding)

10 oz of ricotta or homemade unsalted cream cheese, 3 oz of sugar, 3 oz of ground almonds and 2 or 3 crushed bitter almonds, 5 egg whites, lemon peel, breadcrumbs.

Sieve the cream cheese, add the sugar, the almonds, the beaten whites of eggs and the grated peel of a lemon. Pour into a buttered, 2–2½-pint shallow cake tin, spread breadcrumbs on the top and cook for 30 minutes in a moderate oven.

Enough for six or seven people.

WATERMELON STUFFED WITH BLACKBERRIES

If by any chance you happen to come upon a watermelon and some blackberries in the same season, try this dish.

Cut the watermelon in half, take away the black seeds and cut up the red flesh into pieces. Squeeze lemon juice on to it and mix it with some blackberries. Put them back in the halves of melon, add sugar and put on the ice.

TORTA DI ALBICOCCHE

(Apricot Tart)

Make a pastry with 7 oz of flour, 3½ oz of butter, 3½ oz of vanilla sugar, the yolks of 2 eggs, the grated peel of a small lemon, ½ teacupful of water.

Knead the pastry very lightly and roll it out as little as possible.

Spread it on flat buttered pie tins. Two 6-inch tins are about right. Or use 5 oz flour to 2½ of butter, and about 1 lb of apricots to fill one 8-inch tin.

On top of the pastry arrange 2 lb of apricots which have been cooked with a little sugar, cut into halves and stoned. There should not be too much juice or the pastry will be sodden.

Cook for 25 minutes – the first 15 minutes in a hot oven and the last 10 with the heat diminished. Serve cold.

A most delicious sweet. The vanilla sugar is important to the flavour.

ISABEL ALLENDE · *Voices in My Ear*

NICHOLSON BAKER · *Playing Trombone*

LINDSEY BAREHAM · *The Little Book of Big Soups*

KAREN BLIXEN · *From the Ngong Hills*

DIRK BOGARDE · *Coming of Age*

ANTHONY BURGESS · *Childhood*

ANGELA CARTER · *Lizzie Borden*

CARLOS CASTANEDA · *The Sorcerer's Ring of Power*

ELIZABETH DAVID · *Peperonata and Other Italian Dishes*

RICHARD DAWKINS · *The Pocket Watchmaker*

GERALD DURRELL · *The Pageant of Fireflies*

RICHARD ELLMANN · *The Trial of Oscar Wilde*

EPICURUS · *Letter on Happiness*

MARIANNE FAITHFULL · *Year One*

KEITH FLOYD · *Hot and Spicy Floyd*

ALEXANDER FRATER · *Where the Dawn Comes Up Like Thunder*

ESTHER FREUD · *Meeting Bilal*

JOHN KENNETH GALBRAITH · *The Culture of Contentment*

ROB GRANT AND DOUG NAYLOR · *Scenes from the Dwarf*

ROBERT GRAVES · *The Gods of Olympus*

JANE GRIGSON · *Puddings*

SOPHIE GRIGSON · *From Sophie's Table*

KATHARINE HEPBURN · *Little Me*

SUSAN HILL · *The Badness Within Him*

ALAN HOLLINGHURST · *Adventures Underground*

BARRY HUMPHRIES · *Less is More Please*

HOWARD JACOBSON · *Expulsion from Paradise*

P. D. JAMES · *The Girl Who Loved Graveyards*

STEPHEN KING · *Umney's Last Case*

LAO TZU · *Tao Te Ching*

DAVID LEAVITT · *Chips Is Here*

LAURIE LEE · *To War in Spain*

PATRICK LEIGH FERMOR · *Loose as the Wind*

ELMORE LEONARD · *Trouble at Rindo's Station*

DAVID LODGE · *Surprised by Summer*

BERNARD MAC LAVERTY · *The Miraculous Candidate*

SHENA MACKAY · *Cloud-Cuckoo-Land*

NORMAN MAILER · *The Dressing Room*

PETER MAYLE · *Postcards from Summer*

JAN MORRIS · *Scenes from Havian Life*

BLAKE MORRISON · *Camp Cuba*

VLADIMIR NABOKOV · *Now Remember*

REDMOND O'HANLON · *A River in Borneo*

STEVEN PINKER · *Thinking in Tongues*

CRAIG RAINE · *Private View*

CLAUDIA RODEN · *Ful Medames and Other Vegetarian Dishes*

HELGE RUBINSTEIN · *Chocolate Parfait*

SIMON SCHAMA · *The Taking of the Bastille*

WILL SELF · *The Rock of Crack As Big As the Ritz*

MARK SHAND · *Elephant Tales*

NIGEL SLATER · *30-Minute Suppers*

RICK STEIN · *Fresh from the Sea*

LYTTON STRACHEY · *Florence Nightingale*

PAUL THEROUX · *Slow Trains to Simla*

COLIN THUBRON · *Samarkand*

MARK TULLY · *Beyond Purdah*

LAURENS VAN DER POST · *Merry Christmas, Mr Lawrence*

MARGARET VISSER · *More than Meets the Eye*

GAVIN YOUNG · *Something of Samoa*

and

Thirty Obituaries from Wisden · SELECTED BY MATTHEW ENGEL

READ MORE IN PENGUIN

For complete information about books available from Penguin and how to order them, please write to us at the appropriate address below. Please note that for copyright reasons the selection of books varies from country to country.

IN THE UNITED KINGDOM: Please write to *Dept. EP, Penguin Books Ltd, Bath Road, Harmondsworth, Middlesex UB7 0DA.*

IN THE UNITED STATES: Please write to *Consumer Sales, Penguin USA, P.O. Box 999, Dept. 17109, Bergenfield, New Jersey 07621-0120.* VISA and MasterCard holders call 1-800-253-6476 to order Penguin titles.

IN CANADA: Please write to *Penguin Books Canada Ltd, 10 Alcorn Avenue, Suite 300, Toronto, Ontario M4V 3B2.*

IN AUSTRALIA: Please write to *Penguin Books Australia Ltd, P.O. Box 257, Ringwood, Victoria 3134.*

IN NEW ZEALAND: Please write to *Penguin Books (NZ) Ltd, Private Bag 102902, North Shore Mail Centre, Auckland 10.*

IN INDIA: Please write to *Penguin Books India Pvt Ltd, 706 Eros Apartments, 56 Nehru Place, New Delhi 110 019.*

IN THE NETHERLANDS: Please write to *Penguin Books Netherlands bv, Postbus 3507, NL-1001 AH Amsterdam.*

IN GERMANY: Please write to *Penguin Books Deutschland GmbH, Metzlerstrasse 26, 60594 Frankfurt am Main.*

IN SPAIN: Please write to *Penguin Books S. A., Bravo Murillo 19, 1° B, 28015 Madrid.*

IN ITALY: Please write to *Penguin Italia s.r.l., Via Felice Casati 20, I-20124 Milano.*

IN FRANCE: Please write to *Penguin France S. A., 17 rue Lejeune, F-31000 Toulouse.*

IN JAPAN: Please write to *Penguin Books Japan, Ishikiribashi Building, 2-5-4, Suido, Bunkyo-ku, Tokyo 112.*

IN GREECE: Please write to *Penguin Hellas Ltd, Dimocritou 3, GR-106 71 Athens.*

IN SOUTH AFRICA: Please write to *Longman Penguin Southern Africa (Pty) Ltd, Private Bag X08, Bertsham 2013.*